PRAY
IT FORWARD

Pastor Jon Enter

Published by Straight Talk Books
P.O. Box 301, Milwaukee, WI 53201
800.661.3311 · timeofgrace.org

Copyright © 2017 Time of Grace Ministry

All rights reserved. This publication may not be copied, photocopied, reproduced, translated, or converted to any electronic or machine-readable form in whole or in part, except for brief quotations, without prior written approval from Time of Grace Ministry.

Unless otherwise indicated, Scripture is taken from THE HOLY BIBLE, NEW INTERNATIONAL VERSION®, NIV®. Copyright © 1973, 1978, 1984, 2011 by Biblica, Inc.® Used by permission. All rights reserved worldwide.

Printed in the United States of America
ISBN: 978-1-942107-26-2

TIME OF GRACE *and* IT ALL STARTS NOW *are registered marks of Time of Grace Ministry.*

About Time of Grace

Time of Grace is for people who want more growth and less struggle in their spiritual walk. The timeless truth of God's Word is delivered through television, print, and digital media with millions of content engagements each month. We connect people to God's grace so they know they are loved and forgiven and so they can start living in the freedom they've always wanted.

To discover more, please visit timeofgrace.org, download our free app at timeofgrace.org/app, or call 800.661.3311.

Help share God's message of grace!

Your generosity and prayer support take the gospel of grace to others through our ministry outreach and help them find the restart with Jesus they need.

Give today at timeofgrace.org/give or by calling 800.661.3311.

Thank you!

Contents

Introduction 4

Pray Like a Boss—The Power of Prayer Is Christ 6

Tweeting God—Prayers From the Heart 14

Frustrated Prayer—God, Why Aren't You Answering? .. 23

When You're Wronged—Double Prayer 29

An Attitude of Gratitude—Thankfulness in Prayer 37

Conclusion 46

Introduction

I love God. Since I can remember, I have loved the Lord. And I love people. "Perfect!" I thought as a sophomore in high school, "I should be a pastor!" You know what I didn't love? Praying. Now don't get me wrong. I loved the concept and command of praying, but I wasn't sure how to do it. Sure, I had memorized prayers I would say out loud. But they didn't penetrate me. I had the Lord's Prayer down. In a moment I could rattle it off without thinking, but that was the problem. I didn't think about the words. I tried. I scolded myself, "This time you're going to make it through without your mind wandering for a moment." Sometimes it worked; many times it didn't. No matter how hard I tried praying memorized prayers, I didn't stay engaged.

During my internship year when I was studying to be a pastor, one of the scariest parts of the worship service for me was the prayer section. I wasn't nervous about reading the written-out prayers. Those were easy and joyful. But when someone would catch me minutes before the service and say something like, "Hey, my grandma is sick. Can you pray for her today?" I would fake my best smile and say, "Sure, of course." Inwardly I was terrified, nearly throwing up on the inside. I didn't know how to pray by myself, making up the content as I stumbled my way forward in prayer. And pray out loud? In front of people? In front of God? I didn't like it. I wasn't comfortable. I avoided it. And I'm not alone. Most Christians aren't pray-out-loud-in-front-of-others people.

To get over my fear and failure of praying publicly, I practiced prayed privately with my newlywed wife. Talk about a bonding experience! I asked, "Okay, Honey. Who do you want me to pray for?" She'd list off five or so people. We'd bow our heads. I'd gulp and start praying. I distinctly remember one time when I finished one of my practice-praying sessions on Debbi, after I had crash-landed a way-too-long and rambling prayer in an exhausted "Amen," my frustrated wife blurted out abruptly, "37!" "Huh?" I spouted back, still in cold sweats. "You had 37 'ums' that time." "Ugh" I sighed. "I'm just no good at this."

Praying out loud in front of people is scary. It's unknown. It's awkward. Until now. In *Pray It Forward*, you will learn a prayer formula that's easy and adaptable to any situation to build up your confidence in praying personally, publicly, and privately. As you implement this prayer into your life, Lord willing, it will unlock a new level of joy in praying as it has for me. Now I love to pray with others! When someone says, "Can you keep me in your prayers?" I pray with them right then and right there using the prayer formula in this book. *Being confident to pray out loud with someone who is hurting moves them forward in their connection to God's grace and moves you forward in your joy of praying.*

Pray Like a Boss—The Power of Prayer Is Christ

"There's an app for that!" Have you heard that phrase? With smartphone technology growing in popularity across our nation, entrepreneurs are feverishly working to create the next best app for you to download. Did you know that the people from Rovio who introduced us to the app for Angry Birds—the game where you shoot animated birds in a slingshot at different targets—now have a net worth of over $6 billion! The company that invented the app game Candy Crush is reportedly worth around $7 billion! The success of these two companies and the many others who have tried their hand at inventing apps is the reason why there are currently over 1.2 million apps to choose from. No wonder why "there's an app for that!"

Apps are supposed to make your life better by solving a need you have no matter how big or small—like when you're listening to a song but you can't remember the name and it's driving you nuts . . . there's an app for that called Shazam. Simply hold your phone to the radio, and it'll tell you the artist and song and, of course, give you the option of buying that song from iTunes. Some apps are ridiculous and worthless like the app that tells you how good of a kisser you are. Seriously, there's an app for that. Simply download the app and start kissing the germ-filled face of your phone and it will rate your smooching skills. Other apps are incredibly useful because they solve a problem you have in your life.

In this chapter, we're addressing a problem we all have. It's a problem we don't mean to have, but it's one that happens to even the most faithful Christians—it happens to you . . . telling someone you'll pray for them and then not following through. It's not like you intended to forget. You just did. It happened. There are times you told someone at church you'd pray for them, but you couldn't remember who it was or what it was about. There are other times you told someone you'd pray, and you never thought of it again. In the Christian community, when someone is hurting we say, "I'll pray for you." But sometimes it's something we say more than we do. How sad.

> How truly comforting it is to have someone tell you unexpectedly that they are specifically praying for you.

Concerned Christians have developed dozens of different free downloadable apps to help you fulfill your prayer promises. Yes, there's an app for that—for your prayer life.

From personal experience, I can tell you how truly comforting it is to have someone tell you unexpectedly that they are specifically praying for you. For years, my wife and I saved a message on our answering machine from a pastor who served on the other coast of Florida. He left a simple message on our machine, letting us know that he remembered us that day in prayer. How cool is that? It was so touching, so encouraging, so fulfilling of Christ's command that he gave to pray for and with one another.

We all need prayers. There's a lot of crazy out there! There's a lot of pain we endure on this broken planet. To drive home the point on how God wants us to remember to pray, I'm going to give you two different scenarios when prayer is needed for someone.

Scenario 1—Jim was in extreme pain after a deep cut he suffered while working at an auto repair shop became severely infected. It got so bad he had to be admitted to the hospital in order to save his leg. Jim's primary care doctor, who also worked at the hospital, came to visit him and had the antibiotics Jim needed. But Jim's doctor didn't personally give him the medicine because he oftentimes had trouble opening the packaging and didn't want to look bad in front of Jim. The doctor had every intention of asking a nurse to administer the medication, but he forgot. When Jim asked when he would finally receive his medication, the hospital records showed the meds were given to him even though the doctor forgot. It took many pain-filled hours to correct the problem.

Could you imagine if that happened to you?! If you were Jim, would you really care if the doctor struggled opening the package or just care that you got the medicine you so desperately needed? The doctor forgot to give someone who was in pain the relief he needed because the doctor was concerned he might—*might*—look bad! That's sad. You'd be so upset if that happened to you.

Scenario 2—Jim was in extreme pain after a deep cut he suffered while working at an auto repair shop became severely infected. It got so bad he had to be admitted to the hospital in order to save his leg. You work with Jim's mom, Angie, and through tears Angie told you how worried she was. If Jim lost his leg, he wouldn't be able to work as a mechanic and she didn't know how Jim would be able to make his mortgage payment and support his wife and two children. With care and concern for your coworker friend and the pain she was experiencing for her son, you told her, "I'll pray for you." But then you didn't; you walked away and forgot. You had every intention, but it slipped your mind.

Now, how different are you from the doctor in the first scenario? You both had a means to bring relief—the doctor using medicine; you using prayer to Jesus the Great Physician. You both had perfect intentions of bringing relief but forgot. It slipped your mind. You both missed an opportunity to show love and concern.

There are times when we tell someone we'll pray and don't. What stops us from praying right then and there? The reason why many Christians aren't spontaneous, out-loud praying people is because we're so concerned about looking strange praying in public or looking foolish because we might—*might*—struggle and stumble over our words while praying. Just like the doctor who thought he might—*might*—struggle opening the medicine. Isn't that sad? Self-consciousness keeps us from prayer.

In 1 Corinthians chapter 2, Paul tells us that the power of prayer and the power of communicating to another person the peace of Christ do not rest on the power of our words. They are found only in the power of God! **"I came to you in weakness with great fear and trembling. My message and my preaching were not with wise and persuasive words, but with a demonstration of the Spirit's power"** (verses 3,4). Paul approached the hip and happening city of Corinth—a city that was wowed by wisdom and loved listening to powerful, persuasive preachers—in weakness, in fear, in trembling. The words he spoke were not silky smooth, but they were words heard both by the people and by God!

What would you rather have? Someone pray for you and stumble a bit while praying or someone who said they'd pray but didn't pray at all? The choice is simple! The answer is clear! You'd want someone to pray for you no matter what it sounded like. What you want is what others want from you, for you to pray with them . . . out loud. Right then. Right there.

You might worry and wonder: "How? What do I say?" The answer is found in Paul's words: **"For I resolved to know nothing while I was with you except Jesus Christ and him crucified so that your faith might not rest on human wisdom, but on God's power"** (1 Corinthians 2:2,5). There was one thing and one thing only that Paul focused on while he lived and worked and prayed among the Corinthian people: Jesus. On Christ alone his hope was found. Christ was his Light, his Strength, his All, his Cornerstone, his Solid Ground, firm through the fiercest drought and storm. Knowing and loving Jesus was the only wisdom Paul needed when he prayed and preached.

That's all you need too! If you have faith in Jesus, if you can call upon Jesus' name in prayer, you can pray. But before you can feel comfortable praying out loud for others, pray for yourself.

> *If you have faith in Jesus, if you can call upon Jesus' name in prayer, you can pray.*

"Jesus, empty me that I may be filled with you. Amen." Empty us of our sins. Empty us of being scared to pray for others. Empty us of being so concerned about what we might sound like praying that we then don't immediately pray for others. "Lord Jesus, empty us, forgive us, that we may be filled with you. Amen."

And he has! Christ has filled you! He has filled you full of his grace. He has forgiven you and calms your fears. He reminds you that anything you ask in his name he hears and answers. He reminds you to cast all anxieties on him because he cares for you. If he loves you enough to sacrifice himself on a cross, don't you think he cares enough to hear and answer your prayers even if you stumble and stutter a little? Of course he does! He is full of mercy. He is full of love. He fills you with his grace, his mercy, his forgiveness, and his love for others.

And he has filled you with the ability to pray like a boss, to pray with complete and total confidence because the power of prayer doesn't rest on you; it rests on Christ's power. And you know that power full well. You know what it's like to be healed of your hurt by his forgiveness. You know what it's like to be lifted up from the pit of sadness by his grace. You know what it's like to be overjoyed at his overwhelming goodness. You know Jesus. You know his mercy. You know his grace. And that's all you need to know in order to pray. Just one name—Jesus!

When you say you'll pray, PRAY RIGHT THEN!

How do you pray like a boss?

When you say you'll pray, PRAY! Write a note. Send yourself an email reminder. Use a prayer app like Echo Prayer or Prayer Notes to remind you so you don't forget. Or, better yet . . .

When you say you'll pray, PRAY RIGHT THEN! Pray right there. Then you won't forget. This is the prayer formula for how to pray confidently. Say the person's name and look him or her in the eye to make it personal. "Angie." Now you have that person's deep attention. Then call on Jesus' name in a simple yet powerful prayer: "May Jesus empty you of your worry and fill you with his peace as Jesus cares for your son. Amen." Short. Powerful. Meaningful. All because you spoke Jesus' name and let the power of prayer rest in his power and not your own.

This prayer has such power because of the One to whom you are praying! This prayer formula brings confidence because it is a fill-in-the-blank way to pray but also because God promises to answer any and all of our prayers. "May Jesus empty you of your _____ and fill you with _____. Amen." Simply fill in the first blank with the problem that's afflicting the person, and fill in the second blank with what he or she needs instead to be provided by the Lord.

That's the kind of prayer you can pray daily. That's the kind of prayer you can pray with confidence. The next time someone tells you how his or her heart is hurting and you say, "I'll pray for you," then pray! Join your hearts together in that moment in prayer before your powerful, merciful, and mighty Lord Jesus. Never doubt what one prayer can do! Jesus is answering those prayers but only if you remember to pray them. So pray. Pray with confidence. Pray right then and there.

Tweeting God—Prayers From the Heart

You know how elections go, right? Campaign ads fill the TV airwaves, our mailboxes, and radio ad space, and they're just about everywhere you turn. Talk for this candidate. Talk against that candidate. Talk. Talk. Talk. All this talking seems to be counterproductive; it almost makes you want to stop listening. Oftentimes lots and lots of words just become unproductive words.

Politicians understand how to use lots of words to say very little on the campaign trail. And it continues when they get into office. In fact, they have a word for it: *filibuster*. A filibuster is when a politician who has the Senate floor (i.e., is speaking about an issue that is up for vote) refuses to stop talking in order to try to stop the vote. The rules of a filibuster are simple: you can't stop talking, you can't take bathroom breaks, and there can be no long pauses. Lots of words are spoken with very little meaning.

The longest single-person filibuster in U.S. Senate history was made by Strom Thurmond of South Carolina, who spoke for 24 hours and 18 minutes straight against the Civil Rights Act of 1957. He started at 8:54 P.M. on August 28 and didn't stop until 9:12 P.M. the next evening. He recited the Declaration of Independence, the Bill of Rights, and President George Washington's Farewell

Address, among other historical documents. Other people who have attempted long-winded and long-worded filibusters have read the phone book or recited ingredients in favorite recipes. In the end, most filibusters don't work and actually cost the taxpayers more money in order to keep the Senate chamber open all night for these one-sided "debates." How pointless! In fact, Strom Thurmond's record-breaking filibuster didn't stop the vote. It passed anyway, and public schools across the nation were desegregated and became intergraded.

Jesus calls it pointless when people think they can filibuster God—when they try to stop him from doing his will with their long-winded and long-worded prayers. Jesus calls it pointless when people think they can overpower God with their masterfully worded prayers, as if flowery words; free-flowing sentence structure; tightly worded phrases; and rhyming words coupled with variances in tempo, inflection, and volume will so wow God that he has no choice but to answer yes to their every request. God does not base the value of a prayer on the number of words spoken or whether or not the prayer is smooth sounding. God values the heart of the person praying, not that person's tongue.

> God values the heart of the person praying, not that person's tongue.

Here's what he says in Mathew 5:5-8: **"When you pray, do not be like the hypocrites, for they love to pray standing in the synagogues and on the street corners to be seen by others. Truly I tell you, they have received their reward in full. But when you pray, go into your room, close the door and pray to your Father, who is unseen. Then your Father, who sees what is done in secret, will reward you. And when you pray, do not keep on babbling like pagans, for they think they will be heard because of their many words. Do not be like them, for your Father knows what you need before you ask him."**

So when you pray to God, **"do not keep on babbling like pagans, for they think they will be heard because of their many words."** A pagan is someone who prays to a false god, a made-up god. Those who worshiped false gods in Jesus' day are just like those who pray to false gods today. They think by the length and number of their prayers they will impress their god; he will have to act.

This was the exact scene that happened with the prophets of the false god Baal when they had their fireball showdown with Elijah on Mount Carmel. Do you remember this Old Testament account in Scripture? On one side of the mountaintop were the 450 prophets of Baal. On the other side was only Elijah, who believed in and trusted in the true and only triune God. In the middle were the people of Israel, who didn't know whom to follow so they tuned in to find out who really was and is in control of the universe. Both sides built an altar to their god/God and placed an animal sacrifice on top. Then both prayed to their god/God to have him light the fire. The rules were simple, whichever god/God spontaneously started the sacrifice on fire was the real God.

The false prophets went first. From morning until noon they prayed with many words, hoping they would impress their false god into action. It didn't work because he didn't exist. At noon Elijah started to taunt them: **"'Shout louder!' he said. 'Surely he is a god! Perhaps he is deep in thought, or busy, or traveling. Maybe he is sleeping and must be awakened.' So they shouted louder and slashed themselves with swords and spears, as was their custom, until their blood flowed"** (1 Kings 18:27,28).

Thank you, Lord, that you hear each and every one of our prayers!

What if that's how the triune God had us pray to him? Imagine if you had to pray for hours and hours without end in order to wake God up and possibly have him hear you! Thank you, Lord, that you hear each and every one of our prayers! Worse yet, what if we had to pray like the prophets of Baal who slashed themselves? Imagine if every time you were in worship and the pastor said, "Let us pray . . ." you would immediately pull out your pocket prayer knife and slash yourself until the blood flowed! How pointless! How ridiculous! But that was their custom.

Elijah called the people over to his side. He repaired the altar. He placed the sacrifice on top. He then built a trench around the altar. Three times he had water poured onto it so that it soaked the sacrifice and filled the trench with water. And then Elijah prayed a simple prayer to God. **"Answer me, Lord, answer me, so these people will know that you, Lord, are God, and that you are turning their hearts back again"** (1 Kings 18:37). Simple, right? Nothing fancy. He didn't try to wow God with his words. He simply brought his request to God. And God answered!

God sent a fireball from his hand, and it burned up the sacrifice, the wood, the stones, the soil, and also licked up the water in the trench! God answered this simple prayer in a big way. Not because of Elijah's fancy words but because of Elijah's focused heart that trusted in God.

Elijah's prayer was so short that he could have tweeted it! Elijah didn't pull out his smartphone on Mount Carmel, but he did send out a prayer that was short and sweet—like a tweet. If you don't know how Twitter works and are confused about what a Tweet is . . . a Tweet is a short message sent over social media that is less than 140 characters long. This means tweets are short and to the point. God delights in prayers that are the same! Long or short, fancy words don't impress him; focused hearts do!

Now it might relieve you to know God delights

in prayers that are focused on him and not on fancy words. "Whew, you mean my prayers to God don't have to sound like a trained pastor who sounds so silky smooth and motivational? Whew, you mean if I use improper grammar or if I don't use churchy-sounding words like *sanctify* and *justify* in my prayers, God is still pleased?" Yes! Yes, he is! He is thrilled when you pray like you. Talk the way you usually talk when you prayer to God. Then your prayers are genuine. Otherwise, they'd be awkward, which keeps you from praying, which God doesn't want. He wants you, the real you, in prayer.

> He wants you, the real you, in prayer.

I'm guessing very few of us struggle like the Pharisees did in Jesus' day. I'm just guessing very few if any of us stand on street corners or in the break room at work and pray loudly in front of others with many fancy-worded prayers. When was the last time you prayed out loud in front of someone else so they could hear how righteous you are? I'm guessing pretty much never, right? That's not much of a struggle for us. Proud, self-promoting prayers aren't our demise.

Do you know what is? Feeling inadequate and unworthy to pray. We hear others pray on TV or at church or with our friends, and we think we aren't doing it right. We think if our prayers don't sound silky smooth, then they probably aren't as God-pleasing or as good.

That's the devil whispering in your ear, trying to get you to make prayer about comparing yourself to others. Don't fall for it! Don't listen to it! Prayer is a personal conversation with God. Talk to God in prayer like you'd talk to your best friend about something going on in your life. You'd never call up your friend and sound all fluffy and wordy while you're talking to him or her about what's going on. So why would you think Jesus—the Friend of sinners—wants you to approach him in a fake way, talking in a way that isn't you?

Jesus assures you that when you pray to him, confessing the ways you have sinned against him or when you confess your personal prayer life isn't as strong as it could be or should be, he is merciful. Jesus is forgiving. Jesus is healing. And when you confess how you have disappointed him, remember that God is not impressed with empty words. You aren't commanded to grovel and go on and on and on about how horrible of a sinner you are. God knows your heart; he knows your sorrow. Simply confess that sorrow and ask for his forgiveness. And he will hear and heal.

> You can pray anytime, anywhere, bringing your every request, care, and concern to the Lord.

When you do, the mercy of the Lord will destroy the guilt and eternal consequences of those sins with the same might and fury as when God answered Elijah's prayer. God hears your prayers, and he answers. He reacts. He burns up your past sins with his powerful, unstoppable grace. He never slumbers or sleeps because he knows your needs never cease. He fulfills those needs. He loves your prayers as he loves you. He cherishes your prayers as he cherishes you. Through your personal prayer life, God gives you the joy and the ability to empty from yourself your greatest concerns and know that he will take care of them for your blessing and good. When you pray prayers that aren't filled with wordy fluff, you can bring more concerns to God to be handled by your loving Lord in heaven.

Now just because Jesus taught us in his Word that we don't have to be long-winded and long-worded in our prayers doesn't mean our prayer lives should be shorter. It doesn't mean we should pray less. On the contrary, it frees us to pray more! You can pray anytime, anywhere, bringing your every request, care, and concern to the Lord. You can and are called on by God to follow the example of Jesus, who took time out to simply pray—to dedicate part of your day to being with God in prayer.

I want to close this chapter with a great guide to help you bring many prayers to God. Hold up your hand.

Thumb—Since it is the closest finger, pray for those closest to you.

Pointer—Pray for those in conflict against you or against others.

Middle—Pray for those who rose to power in your life/church/country.

Ring—Pray for those in marriage, dating, divorcing, or lonely.

Pinky—Pray for those who are weakened, belittled, or helpless.

Use this "handheld guide to prayer" to open up your personal prayer life. Cast all your anxieties on him. Cast all your cares on him. Pray without ceasing to the God of the impossible and see what God will make possible in your life!

Frustrated Prayer—God, Why Aren't You Answering?

In the last chapter we learned God wants us to pray from our hearts of faith—and he promises to listen to all of our prayers. But what about those times when it seems as though he *isn't* listening or at least not answering? Then what?

Why won't God just make it better? You love him. You live for him. You want your life to please him. And yet despite his mercy-filled love and despite your faith-driven response to his love, there are parts of your life that hurt your heart . . . it just isn't getting better. The ache remains. The pain is pulsing. Oh, you've prayed. You've asked for help. You've asked for healing. You've asked for God to act. And yet, nothing. It remains. Should you keep praying over and over again, or is it time to pack up that prayer because God isn't answering? There are times when we are locked up in frustrated prayer. So what do we do when God says no?

When Moses prayed to God to release his people from slavery in Egypt, he got a no from God at a time when Moses expected God to act. Talk about a frustrated prayer! Read this:

"Moses returned to the Lord and said, 'Why, Lord, why have you brought trouble on this people? Is this why you sent me? Ever since I went to Pharaoh to speak in your name, he has brought trouble on this people, and you have not

rescued your people at all'" (Exodus 5:22,23).

This all started as Moses was tending sheep. He saw a strange sight—a bush on fire that didn't burn up. When Moses went over to investigate, a voice boomed forth from the burning bush. It was God. God called Moses to go to Pharaoh and tell him God's message: "Let my people go!" At first, Moses refused. But God can be quite persuasive. So Moses went.

Armed with a couple miracles that God gave him and with the assurance he was doing the Lord's will, Moses stood toe-to-toe with the world's most powerful man and demanded him to do something he didn't want to do: "Let God's people go. You have no choice, Pharaoh. God has spoken to me and you must let your free labor force leave."

Moses did his miracles. He tucked his hand into his cloak, pulled it out, and it was diseased. He put it back in again, and when he pulled it out, it was healed. "That should convince him," Moses thought. Then, to seal the deal, Moses threw his staff on the ground just as God told him to do and it turned into a snake. "That should do it!" Moses smiled with confidence. Then Moses hit Pharaoh with God's one-sided decree: "Pharaoh, God says, 'Let my people go.'" Moses waited for Pharaoh to crumble to his knees, cry out in fear, and grant God's command. But he didn't. That's not what happened. Rather than a yes, Moses heard NO!

Pharaoh refused. Because Moses confronted him, Pharaoh made the Israelites' life of slavery even worse. They were no longer given straw as the bonding agent in the bricks they made; they had to collect the straw from the fields and still make just as many bricks. When they didn't—because it was impossible—they were beaten. Some Israelites found Moses and told him off, **"May the Lord look on you and judge you! You have made us obnoxious to Pharaoh and his officials and have put a sword in their hand to kill us"** (Exodus 5:21).

Moses was baffled, perplexed, hurt, confused, and even a bit angry at God. After all, he didn't want to do this in the first place! And when he did exactly what God told him to do, it didn't work. Life got worse. So he prayed to God in frustration, **"Why, Lord, why have you brought trouble on this people? Is this why you sent me? . . . You have not rescued your people at all"** (Exodus 5:22,23).

How frustrating! Moses was faithful. He loved God. He was living for God. He wanted his life to please God. And even though he did exactly what God asked him to do, his life got worse.

Moses did what was right. He proclaimed what God told him. Yet he didn't see God acting in his life. He spoke frustrated prayers, wondering what happened, what went wrong, what should he have done differently for God to act?

I'm certain there have been times when you wondered, "Whoa, what happened?" You were left wondering why God allowed something so unpleasant or so horrible to happen in your life, especially when you didn't do anything wrong to cause it. When we do wrong, when we break God's laws, we understand God sends a natural consequence to that spiritual sin. We know God is perfectly fair and just. But what about when God doesn't seem to be fair? What about when you do what God commands—at least you have lived according to your faith as best as you are able, dedicating yourself to Jesus—and all of a sudden life derails . . . what about then? The path and plan are gone, totally demolished, and you're left wondering what happened.

You prayed to God for a way out. You prayed to God for peace. You prayed to God for deliverance, but he didn't answer. The pain remained and only seemed to get worse. When that happens—and it does—you end up getting locked up in frustrated prayer. It's frustrating because you know God loves you and promises to watch over you, but you simply aren't seeing God's response.

When you're locked in frustrated prayer, the devil is right there licking his chops to sink his teeth into your soul and your trust in God. "God doesn't care about you," he sneers and whispers. "If he did, he would've done something by now. Maybe he doesn't love you or maybe you need to earn his favor in order for him to act or maybe, just maybe, he doesn't even exist. After all, where is he? He's not helping you!"

Those lies are so easy to believe when you're in pain. Those lies are so easy to believe when you know God could do something to make it all go away and he doesn't. So what do you do?

Trust God's will! When we hear a no from God, *it's not a rejection; it's a redirection.* God's definition of blessing us is different from ours. Our definition of a blessing is when he makes life easy, effortless, and engulfed in earthly goodness.

God's definition of blessing is positioning us so our eyes are fixed in faith on his Son as our Savior. That means there will be life lessons we can only learn by having tough times and surviving the test through Jesus. That means there will be times we have more than we can handle so we have no choice but to rely on Christ's mercy, guidance, and love. That means there will be times when we pray and don't hear his response or see him working right away so we listen for him more closely and search his will more fervently.

> *When God says no, it means he has something bigger, better planned.*

Think of it this way: a teacher is always quiet DURING a test, but that doesn't mean the teacher isn't there. And there are other times when God answers our prayers in such abundance we can do nothing more than marvel at the amazing bounty of his goodness as our cup overflows!

When God says no, it means he has something bigger, better planned. When Jesus prayed to his Father in heaven, asking if there was another way to save the world that didn't involve the pathway of pain through the cross, through hell, God the

Father said no. That no from the Father brought unimaginable blessings to the world.

God always hears. God always answers our prayers. And he always—always, without doubt, always—answers our prayers for our good, for our grace, for our eternal blessing. When you're frustrated in your prayers because you don't see or hear or feel God responding, wait on his will. Continue to trust. God might be answering no to your prayers in order to bring a bigger blessing, to bring a bigger yes later. God might be answering no to your prayers in order to have you fully appreciate the yes he will give you when the time is right.

If God had not answered no to Moses' frustrated prayer, which caused Pharaoh to make the Israelites' lives worse, then the Israelite people wouldn't have seen the obvious signs of God's power. They would've struggled to place their trust in him. God knew what he was doing; he was drawing them into a deeper relationship with him.

God knows what he is doing in your life too, even if you don't understand his will or his plan. Keep praying. Keep trusting. God's delays are not always denials. God has a plan for you in your life to get you through any and all pain for one purpose—to draw you closer to him in faith. God's no is not a rejection; it's a redirection . . . directing you deeper into his grace!

When You're Wronged—Double Pray

Is there someone in your life whom—if you had the option—you would rather never see again? Who makes your skin crawl, your blood boil, your annoyance meter flash WARNING, WARNING, WARNING LOWLIFE APPROACHING! Whom do you wish was out of your life because you're done with the drama, done with the lying and manipulation, done with the heartache constantly caused by him or her?

Do you have that person's face locked in your mind? The one who seems to enjoy causing you pain and discomfort. The one who seems to contradict you at every turn. The one who has caused you more pain than he or she probably even knows. This chapter is about you and that person. This chapter is about what to do when people do spiteful, vengeful, and regretful things against you that they simply don't regret. What do you do? Is it okay to pray for justice, for God to give them a taste of their own medicine, to pray that God will punish them to set them straight and teach them a lesson? Is that wrong?

Is it okay to pray for justice?

To answer that question, let's talk a little bit about Stephen. You know, the guy in the Bible. I'm certain Stephen had quite a number of faces of people he wished would leave his life—like the ones who were stoning him to death! We know very little about Stephen, but his life and death teach us a great deal. In Acts chapter 2, the apostle Peter addressed a curious crowd in Jerusalem, preaching and teaching to them the pure message of Jesus' grace. By day's end, the Holy Spirit brought three thousand people to faith in Jesus. Just two chapters later in the book of Acts, the number of believers who came to faith in Jerusalem was five thousand men, plus presumably a great number of women and children.

Needless to say, this boom of believers created a logistical problem for organizing and leading the early Christian church. What a great problem to have, right? It was a problem they solved by selecting seven men to organize and lead the day-to-day operations of the church. One of those seven men was Stephen, who was described as a man **"full of the Spirit and wisdom"** (Acts 6:3).

Stephen was a righteous man. A good guy. A guy who would give you the shirt off his back. The kind of good neighbor who would lend you any tool, help you with any project anytime. Stephen was the kind of guy who—when you sneezed out in public—would say, "God bless you" with a ready smile. He was a good guy who loved God and loved God's people. So why did people throw rocks at his head and body until he died?

Stephen did nothing wrong! He simply told the Jewish leadership what they had done—they had rejected and killed Jesus, which they knew. And he proclaimed Jesus to be the Savior of the world, which he is. They rushed at him, grabbed him, dragged him outside of the city, and picked up rocks and stones to whip at his body with all their anger-filled might.

He did nothing wrong, and yet he was attacked. Sound familiar? Sometimes it happens in the simplest of ways when you do nothing wrong and yet get wronged by the person who uses her shopping cart at Walmart like a battering ram to shove and push her way in front of you in line. Clearly you were waiting in the slowest moving checkout line on earth! And yet she butted and busted her way in. And when you said, "Excuse me, I was here." She unleashed on you an assault of anger.

It happens on city streets or even on the freeway, but rather than using a shopping cart, it's a couple thousand pound car that some pushy person is using like a weapon. It happens when you hesitate for .10 seconds after a red light turns green and suddenly . . . HOOOOOOOOOOONK! The driver behind you blasts the horn because you didn't have the reaction time of a professional drag racer while sitting in your minivan. "Sorry, pal!" you respond while reaching back to pick up the stuffed animal your child dropped and won't stop screaming until it is back in her arms. "Fluffy bunny hit the floor. Lay off the horn and try switching to decaf!"

When you get to work, the unhappiness

continues; the mistreatment is almost expected. Your boss demands more than is humanly possible and doesn't seem to appreciate all your hard work and dedication. Why? Because your coworker is quick to take credit for everything and anything but is also quick to slack off when no one's looking . . . and who gets to pick up the slack when that happens? You do! You get stuck with the extra work! Is there a thank-you? Of course not.

When you get home, it's more of the same. When something goes wrong, it's your fault. If you do something, it's done wrong. If you say something, you say it wrong. If you don't say something, even that's wrong. You don't live up to the expectations of your in-laws. You don't measure up to your golden-boy brother, or your sassy sister always has something to say. And then there's the noisy neighbor who just won't stop thumping the music or talking/yelling/cussing on the phone outside late at night so you can't sleep.

What did you do wrong to deserve this mistreatment? Nothing. You existed. You were. You are. But they don't seem to notice how annoying, how selfish, how hurtful they are to you. They won't stop. They don't stop. Is it okay to pray to God to make them stop, to give them a nonlethal but painful dose of their own medicine, to pray that God will punish them to set them straight and teach them a lesson? Is that wrong?

Let's ask Jesus. If ever there was someone who was mistreated, who deserved no vile evil against him, it was the perfect Son of God. Jesus prescribes for us how we are to react to unfair mistreatment:

"You have heard that it was said, 'Eye for eye, and tooth for tooth.' But I tell you, do not resist an evil person. If anyone slaps you on the right cheek, turn to them the other cheek also. If anyone forces you to go one mile, go with them two miles" (Matthew 5:38,39,41).

If ever there was someone who was mistreated, who deserved no vile evil against him, it was the perfect Son of God.

Jesus' society was just like ours. Our society today teaches, "If you don't want someone to mistreat you, hit them harder than they hit you." An eye for an eye. Jesus tells you that's not how your heavenly Father wants you to live. Not in vengeance. Not in revenge. Not in steaming, sulking anger. Turn the other cheek. Rise above by not sinking down to that level.

If someone forces you to do something, go above and beyond that person's expectation, doing it not for their glory but to glorify the Father in whose name you are acting. Under Roman law, any Roman soldier could force a Jewish person to carry his burdensome soldier's pack for a mile. Jesus said, "Go for two miles." Don't react in anger; react in abundant love. If you fight fire with fire, you'll only have a bigger fire. Fight someone's fiery mistreatment of your life with something else;

with the soothing, extinguishing love of Christ. It may or may not change them, but it will change you. It will bring you peace in the midst of peril.

Jesus continued with one final command. A command fulfilled by Stephen. Jesus taught, **"You have heard that it was said, 'Love your neighbor and hate your enemy.' But I tell you, love your enemies and pray for those who persecute you"** (Matthew 5:43,44). This is exactly what Stephen did as he was unfairly and unjustly being stoned to death. He didn't cry out to God for justice. He didn't pray to God to send a fireball from heaven to destroy his attackers. He didn't pray against them; he prayed for them. **"Lord, do not hold this sin against them"** (Acts 7:60).

When you're wronged, double pray.

When you're wronged, don't just turn the other cheek but turn the mirror. What? When we're wronged, we're quick to complain about how others mistreated us and show them their actions and how they wronged us. Turn the mirror. Examine yourself. Ask how you may have contributed to their actions. Ask how you've reacted. Did you declare yourself judge and jury and now are asking God in prayer to be the executioner of your revenge?

When you're wronged, double pray. Pray for forgiveness of your reaction and pray to God to forgive their action.

You may not have deserved how you were treated, but how you reacted was far from holy, righteous, and God-pleasing. Sin never justifies sin. Two wrongs don't make a right—it makes both people more engulfed in the guilt of their sins. There are two types of people; which one are you? When you're mistreated, do you fight or take flight? Do you react in anger and fight back with your words and actions? If so, you break God's heart. You sin. Or do you take flight and internalize hurtful words and sulk in sadness, have fights with them in your mind: "If that ever happens again, I'm so going to do THIS!" But until that happens, you stew over them and how vile they are. If you do this, you break God's heart. You sin.

Double pray! Pray for forgiveness of your reaction. Neither of those reactions—fight or flight—brings resolve nor do they reflect the words, actions, and love of Jesus. When Jesus was mistreated, when he was placed on trial for sins that were not his, when he was abused and beaten and sentenced to die, he didn't fight back. He didn't take flight. He endured. He brought change by being the change. Christ Jesus freed you and has forgiven you for not rising above; he has forgiven you for sinking low in revenge and retaliation. He took every hateful word you spoke in revenge, every thought you had of retaliation, and every action you did to try to get even, and he paid for them on his cross of love and healing. The hurt you have is healed by his love if you'll only focus on him and not on those who treat you as they did him.

Double pray! Pray for forgiveness of your reaction and pray to God to forgive their loveless actions against you. Just as Stephen prayed, **"Lord, do not hold this sin against them"** (Acts 7:60), just as Jesus prayed, **"Father, forgive them, for they do know not what they are doing"** (Luke 23:34), so also may you pray. Pray for those who hurt you.

Pray for those who hurt you.

If you want a better boss, pray for the boss you have every day.

If you want better employees, pray for those you have every day.

If you want a more loving spouse, pray for your spouse every day.

If you want to get along with your in-laws, pray for them every day.

Double pray! Pray for your heart and for the heart of those who are in conflict against you. It will change how you react to them. And, Lord willing, it will slowly change how they act toward you.

An Attitude of Gratitude— Thankfulness in Prayer

Here's a story one of my church members shared with me. I want to share it with you because it fits the prayer topic that I want to address in this chapter. This story is a modern parable that encourages us to add something particular into our prayer lives.

> I dreamt I went to heaven and an angel was showing me around. We walked side-by-side inside a large workroom filled with angels. My angel guide stopped in front of the first section and said, "This is the Receiving Section. Here is where all prayers sent to God for someone's personal problems are received." I looked around in this area, and it was terribly busy with many angels sorting out petitions written on volumes and volumes of paper from people all over the world.
>
> Then we moved on down a long corridor until we reached the second section. The angel said to me, "This is the Packaging and Delivery Section. Here prayers are processed and delivered when someone on earth prays for another person on earth." I noticed again how busy it was there. There were many angels working hard at that

station, since so many blessings had been requested and were being packaged for delivery to earth.

Finally, at the farthest end of the long corridor we stopped at the door of a very small station. To my great surprise, only one angel was seated there, waiting for the next prayer to arrive. "This is the Acknowledgment Section," my angel friend quietly admitted to me. He seemed embarrassed. "How is it that there is only one angel in here to receive these types of prayers?" I asked.

"It's so sad," the angel sighed. "After people receive the blessings that they asked for, very few send back acknowledgments. Very few thank God for all the blessings he gives—both big and small—most go unthanked and unnoticed."

How sad indeed! We're really good at praying to God for our needs. And we shouldn't be ashamed of that! That's good. That's God-pleasing. Jesus invites those prayers. He wants to hear them and answers them. In no way should we slow down or minimize the amount of times we pray to God, asking for him to intercede in our lives or in the lives of those we care about. But if we were to weigh on a scale the volume of prayers asking for God's help with something and on the other side weigh the prayers said thanking God for his blessings, the scale would tip in one direction, showing how off balance our prayer life is. We pray exceedingly more prayers about *me* and *he* and *she* than we do thanking *Thee*!

It's not that we don't pray prayers of thanks to God for his goodness. Oh, we do. And they are heartfelt, true, and genuine. But they are short-lived. Let me explain this. When we're deeply entrenched in a problem or a pain, we pray continually for that need. We spend days, weeks, even months in prayer continually asking God for help and relief. And when that goodness from God comes, we're overjoyed! Sometimes so overjoyed at the blessing being given that we go enjoy the blessing without thanking the Blesser. Or we are so overjoyed that we drop right to our knees in prayerful thanksgiving. But then that's it. We thanked God—and it was genuine—but then we move on. Wait! Days, weeks, months of prayer asking, "Give me. Give me. Give me." Then he only gets one quick "Thank Thee" prayer? Is that balanced?

We have much to be thankful for! We have a loving Lord who hears our prayers—any time, in every way, every day! We have a mighty Lord who's strong enough to destroy any danger and yet gentle

> **We pray exceedingly more prayers about me and he and she than we do thanking Thee!**

enough to calm any concern. We have a merciful Lord who loves us so much he sent his own Son into the darkness of this world to rescue us. We have a bountiful Lord who blesses us in so many ways that they become commonplace and we don't even see how good we have it.

Sometimes our first-world problems blind us from seeing the struggles happening around the world. Seventy-five percent of people in the world do not have food in the refrigerator and a roof over their heads to sleep at night. Ninety-two percent of people in the world do not have money in the bank, spare cash in their wallets, and spare change sitting in a dish at home. Only one percent of people in the world own their own computers with a Wi-Fi signal in their homes.

Seven hundred million people experience the fear of battle, the loneliness of imprisonment, the agony of torture, or the pangs of starvation. Just by holding your head up and smiling, you're unique to all those in doubt and despair. And more than three billion people go to church with the fear of harassment, arrest, torture, or death.

We have much to be thankful for!

How truly, richly, mind-bogglingly BLESSED we are! We have much to be thankful for! But we don't do the greatest job we can thanking God continually, regularly, and consistently in prayers throughout our day, every day.

Some would argue that God doesn't need it. He

doesn't need or want our specific prayers of thanks because, after all, he knows how thankful we are when he sees us enjoying his blessings. Isn't it thanks enough for God to see us happy with his gifts?

Here's a story from Scripture that answers the question: **"On his way to Jerusalem . . . ten men who had leprosy met him. They stood at a distance and called out in a loud voice, 'Jesus, Master, have pity on us!'"** (Luke 17:11-13). No one else had mercy on these men. No one else could. Leprosy was a highly contagious and incurable skin disease. These men, by law, had to stay a considerable distance away from any healthy person. They cried out for Jesus' pity. And that's what they received. Jesus cared for them. He met their needs, just as he has ours.

"When he saw them, he said, 'Go, show yourselves to the priests.' And as they went, they were cleansed" (Luke 17:14). Notice that Jesus had their healing connected to their actions. Jesus answered their request by having them be active in bringing the relief they needed. If they didn't go to the priests in Jerusalem—which was a long, difficult journey for them—they wouldn't have been healed. As they did the work of going to the priests, healing came. We don't know how long this took, but since their healing wasn't immediate and since they took part in the process of bringing the healing, only one of the ten returned to give thanks. **"One of them, when he saw he was healed, came back, praising God in a loud voice.**

He threw himself at Jesus' feet and thanked him—and he was a Samaritan" (Luke 17:15,16).

Too often that percentage is a glimpse into our own lives of thanks. When we pray for help or healing and the answer to that prayer involves us doing something to bring about the results (doctor visit, health change, be more focused, apologizing), we are less likely to remember to pray to God in thanksgiving. Wait! We prayed to him. We asked him for help. And HE BLESSED our actions, yet our thanksgiving too often slips from our minds because of our involvement. Sometimes God uses you and your efforts as the answer to your prayer. But that doesn't mean he deserves less thanks!

Sometimes God uses you and your efforts as the answer to your prayer.

That's what happened to nine of the ten men cured of leprosy. Because they took part in the action of their healing and because time elapsed since their request of Jesus, they forgot to give him the thanks he deserved. Jesus deserves all of our thanks and praise! Not only does he answer our prayers, but he makes time for us.

That's what he did for these ten men with leprosy. Look carefully at the first few words of Luke 7:11: **"On his way to Jerusalem . . ."** Jesus was on his final approach to Jerusalem to fulfill the prophecies of God's Holy Word for the Holy One to die to make us all free and forgiven. Jesus was on his way to give these ten men a greater gift than healing from their physical disease; Jesus was on his way to heal them permanently from their spiritual disease of sin. His task was much greater; his task was more important. And yet, Jesus took time for them! Jesus stopped what he was doing just for them.

That's the grace and mercy of your loving Lord! Jesus is by his Father's side in heavenly glory. He is actively preparing a place in heaven for all believers. He is joyfully greeting each redeemed soul as they enter into their eternal rest with him. He is ruling over the good of his church for his people, for you. Jesus is busy! Jesus is active. And yet Jesus stops what he is doing and where he is going in heaven to help you, to heal you, to answer your prayers, to fulfill your needs, to bring grace back into your life. Jesus makes you his focused priority when he has everything else to do. He prioritizes you and prospers you with his grace and forgiveness! Are you prioritizing your prayers of thanksgiving to him?

> *Are you prioritizing your prayers of thanksgiving to him?*

What is the worst thing you've done wrong in your life? What is the one act that you're the most ashamed about? The simple thought of that horrible act causes guilt to course up and down your spine right into your soul. Why? Jesus has forgiven that sin! Jesus has righted that wrong! Jesus doesn't want you to feel guilty because he crucified your guilt along with that sin. Jesus wants you to feel thanksgiving! Jesus wants you to shout in joy: "That's not me anymore! Thanks be to God!"

The same is true of that dumb deed you did last week. It's gone! It's forgiven! It's wiped clean from your record. When you confessed it to Jesus, it was crucified with Christ. Praise Jesus for that healing. Raise your praise for his love. Yes, learn from your mistake so you don't do it again, but don't forget to give thanks. Too often we look at forgiven sins as battle scars showing our weakness. NO, THEY ARE NOT! *Forgiven* sins are victory medals of God's mercy and might! They show the depth of God's love for you. They are reminders to have an attitude of gratitude, to pray joy-filled, heart-thumping, soul-soaring prayers of thanksgiving to Jesus!

That attitude of gratitude doesn't just stop in transforming how we look at our past. It changes how we see the problems of our present as well. With every prayer of need we bring to God, we can also include a prayer of thanks. The prayer: "Lord, help me not be late to work" could also include, "Thank you for my job." The prayer: "Lord, give me patience with my coworker who is so snotty she won't talk to me" could also include, "Thank you for that coworker not yelling at me." The prayer: "Lord, help me lose weight" could also include, "Thank you for the abundance I have." The prayer: "Lord, help me through this pain" could also include, "Thank you for being willing to endure the pain of the cross for me."

We have so many reasons to give thanks! May we tip the scales back again so that our lives are filled with the prayers of thanksgiving that Jesus deserves, giving him thanks for all the blessings he pours upon us.

Conclusion

The weekend after I taught my church members to tweet prayers to God, to pray immediately for someone they saw in need, it happened to me, for me. I had a rather hurtful conversation with someone angry at life who took out their pain on me. It just happened. Moments earlier I was the verbal punching bag for someone's repressed, now expressed, anger. Amazingly, God directed it for me to cross paths with a dear friend at church. She saw my hurt. When she asked me what was wrong, I couldn't even speak. My hurting heart spun me into confusion. She used the prayer formula I had just taught her the week before in worship to release me from the prison of pain I was just thrown into. "Pastor Jon" she said with a smile that beamed Jesus' love from her heart of faith, "May Jesus empty you of all the pain that's crushing you and fill you with joy and peace in his great love. Amen." It was amazing! Uplifting! Personally encouraging! The Lord answered her simple prayer, and the Spirit poured peace into my heart. It was what I needed, when I needed it. She prayed it forward.

You hold in your heart the name that is above every name; you have been given faith by the Spirit so you possess the name of Jesus. The God of the Universe. The Savior of the World. The Light that scatters the darkness. The Answer to every problem. Use freely, fully, faithfully the name of

Jesus in your prayer life to pray it forward, to pray others forward into peace and the protection of the Almighty. Bathe your life in prayer. Cover your loved ones in the power of the Almighty. No matter what is threatening you or those you love, God's got this. God's got you. Always. Forever.

About the Writer

Jon Enter serves as a pastor in West Palm Beach, Florida, where he's been for ten years. He has focused on youth ministry to grow his mission church, challenging youth and adults to tear off the perception of perfection—that we as Christians will have our lives perfectly together—and to, instead, be open and honest with the Almighty that we need his grace and guidance. His transparent preaching and energetic teaching have connected with the people of south Florida and beyond. Jon also serves as a part-time host on the *Time of Grace* television program and as a regular speaker on *Your* Time of Grace video devotions. He once led a tour at his college, and the Lord had him meet his future wife, Debbi, and they are now drowning in pink and glitter with their four daughters: Violet, Lydia, Eden, and Maggie.